Cooking Britain

Diana Peacock

Table of Contents

Diana Peacock

Introduction

The UK may be a small group of islands, but what a rich food heritage we own. A great variety of dishes and ingredients from such a small area, encompassing traditional fare and modern recipes influenced by a more recent lifestyle.

There is a resurgence of people demanding fresh food that doesn't have to travel hundreds of miles to reach our table. It should become the normal way of things as it was fifty or sixty years ago. Eating seasonally has also become more popular. I don't want to eat tangerines in the summer or strawberries at Christmas.
We should be very proud of all we have and celebrate Great British food that uses produce sourced locally and seasonally.

This book only touches the surface of the wonderful dishes that have sustained us both in past and present, but gives a 'flavour' of each region that contributes to Great British gastronomy.

A lot of people are disparaging about British food. They consider it somewhat second class, stodgy, unhealthy, unvarying. But they only ever see British fast food which, like almost every fast food around the planet, can be relegated to the gastronomic dustbin.

However, British food, real British food, represents the region it comes from just as importantly as any French Department or Italian province. Moreover, British food has its own history. Take black pudding as an example. The Lancashire peasantry kept pigs for the great monasteries of Whalley and Kirkstall, but all they got to keep from the animal was the blood. Hence blood sausage is still a major fast food at Bury Market and has found its way to the northern version of the national dish: the Full English.

British food is seasonal, local, healthy, cheap and above all, flavoursome. All cooking, wherever it originates, can be made healthier with less salt, less saturated fat and so on. There is nothing about British food that is not improved by modern cooking methodology, but at the same time there is much to learn from the past.

Cooking chicken in a pot of water as opposed to roasting it in an oven, for example, gives three meals rather than one and the time when everyone had an oven in their kitchen actually brought more waste. Precious stock with which to make gravy evaporated away and the dry heat was expensive to maintain.

This book takes you on a journey around the UK and is filled with recipes from the regions that represent it most specifically. You will find some of the old favourites and one or two surprises along the way. More than anything I hope you will find the love for British cooking and actually try the recipes.

Diana Peacock
Rossendale,
Lancashire
2013

Chapter 1

London and the South East

Jellied eels, eel pie and eel and mash were just a few of the dishes served up on barrows on the London streets. This region of Britain has many delicious recipes that warm the 'cockles' of your heart. The South East of the country has a cosmopolitan feel to it these days and, in a way, it always did. Food from all over the country was walked in to London markets, and you could get almost anything from fresh seafood via the Thames to popular country food from around the Home Counties.

With the coming of trains this tendency simply increased and London became a gastronomic Mecca for foodies as well as having a vibrant street food scene which is not often seen these days.

Roast nuts in their season were common on many street corners and the major preoccupation became the adequate feeding of the increasing number of poor people. Consequently fast food came to London.

We didn't invent fast food. That was probably done by the Germans, and particularly the Germans in America, with hamburgers and sausages but we do have some specific contributions that remain quintessentially British - fish and chips and pie and mash shops grew up all over the capital and the rest of the country.

Jellied Eels

Eels, as with any other fish, should be cooked as freshly as possible for the best flavour.

INGREDIENTS

Serves 4

450g fresh eels, cut into 12cm-long pieces
300ml fish stock
1 small onion, finely chopped
1 carrot, diced
1 stick of celery, chopped
1 bouquet garni
10g gelatine
3–4 tsp lemon juice and the grated zest of half a lemon
1 tbsp chopped parsley
1 tsp chopped dill
1 bay leaf
A little grated nutmeg
Salt and pepper to taste
Fresh parsley sprigs to decorate

METHOD
1. Place the eels flesh side up in a large dish and sprinkle over the nutmeg, herbs, lemon juice and zest.
2. Roll the pieces of eel up and secure with string.
3. Put the stock, carrot, onion, celery, bay leaf and bouquet garni into a pan and bring to the boil. Add the eels and turn down the heat to simmering. Cook for 15 minutes.
4. Remove the eels from the stock and untie the string then place them in a dish. Remove the bouquet garni and bay leaf from the stock and measure the liquor.

Make up to 350ml with boiling water if necessary.

5. Stir the gelatine into the hot stock and check for seasoning. Add salt and pepper if necessary.

6. Pour the jellied stock over the fish and leave to cool. When cool place in the fridge to set completely.

7. Serve decorated with fresh parsley.

Eel and Parsley Soup

This is my favourite way of eating eels; it is a very savoury dish. If you prefer, use the same amount of nutmeg in place of the mace.

INGREDIENTS
Serves 6
600ml fish or vegetable stock
600ml water
½ tsp ground mace
1 tsp grated lemon zest
Bouquet garni
Salt and black pepper
450g eels
50g butter
2 onions, chopped finely
2 tbsp flour
200ml milk
50ml dry white wine
2 egg yolks
4 tbsp chopped parsley

METHOD
1. Put the stock, water, mace, lemon zest and the bouquet garni into a pan and season with salt and black pepper. Bring to the boil.
2. When the stock is boiling add the eels and simmer gently for about 20 minutes or until the eels are tender.
3. Remove the fish from the stock, cut into small pieces and set aside. Strain the liquor into a bowl or jug.
4. Heat the butter in a large saucepan and add the onions. Fry them very gently until they are soft.
5. Sprinkle over the flour and gradually stir in the stock, milk and white wine. Stir constantly until everything

thickens. Do this over a gentle heat.

6. Add the fish and the parsley, and heat gently.

7. Beat the egg yolks with 2 tbsp of the soup liquid and stir into the soup quickly. Carry on cooking for 3 minutes on the low heat and serve immediately with hunks of bread.

Omelette 'Arnold Bennett'

This delicious way of serving eggs, Finnan haddock and Parmesan cheese was first prepared for the novelist, Arnold Bennett, in London's Savoy Grill. He would request this dish for breakfast in any hotel he stayed in thereafter. This is a slightly easier version than the original one but is still as tasty.

INGREDIENTS

Serves 2

120g Finnan haddock or any good quality smoked haddock
100ml milk
Salt and pepper
1 dessertspoon of corn flour mixed with 2 tbsp. cold milk
1 tbsp. freshly grated Parmesan cheese
1 tbsp. grated Gruyere cheese
4 eggs
20g butter
2 tbsp. double cream

METHOD

1. Poach the fish in the milk for about 10 minutes. When cooked, lift the fish out into a bowl and flake.
2. Heat the poaching liquid and simmer to reduce slightly. Stir in the corn flour and cook until it thickens. Season to taste. Stir in the cheeses and pour over the fish. Stir gently to mix but not vigorously as the fish will disintegrate.
3. Heat the grill to its hottest setting. Beat the eggs and melt the butter in a large frying pan. Add the eggs when the butter starts to foam. Cook over a medium heat until the omelette is just set but still runny on top.

4. Spoon the fish mixture over the top of the eggs and drizzle over the cream.
5. Place the omelette under the grill and cook until the top begins to brown and bubble. Serve immediately.

Kentish Chicken Pudding

This is almost the chicken version of a steak and kidney pudding using chicken, bacon and mushrooms. Boiling chicken can be used for this recipe or for ease of preparation use boned chicken thighs.

INGREDIENTS

Serves 4–5

1.5kg chicken
350g suet crust pastry
220g chopped bacon
1 onion, chopped finely
100g large mushrooms, sliced thickly
20g butter
20g plain flour
500ml chicken stock
1 tbsp. fresh chopped parsley
Salt and pepper

METHOD

1. Remove the meat from the bones of the chicken and make the stock with them by boiling with salt, pepper and a bouquet garni for 2–3 hours.
2. Grease a 1.5 litre pudding basin and roll out the pastry to line the basin, saving enough pastry to make the lid of the pudding.
3. Chop the chicken into bite-size pieces and place in a bowl.
4. Mix the bacon, onion, mushrooms and parsley with the chicken and pack tightly into the pudding basin.
5. Melt the butter in a pan with the flour and stir together over a low heat.

6. Stir in the stock and bring to the boil. Stir until the mixture thickens. Season with salt and pepper if necessary.
7. Pour sufficient of the sauce into the meat mixture and reserve the other to serve with the cooked pudding.
8. Roll out a lid with the reserved pastry and press firmly on top of the pudding.
9. Cover with a layer of greaseproof paper and a layer of foil and tie securely with string.
10. Steam for 2 hours. Serve with mashed potatoes and the reserved sauce.

The mushrooms may be omitted and replaced with diced Bramley apples for a change.

Portmanteau'd Lamb Chops

A portmanteau was a heavy leather piece of luggage that opened at the top so items to be carried could be removed easily whilst travelling. The chops are sliced through the fat end and stuffed just like a carrying case.

INGREDIENTS

Serves 4

4 thickly cut lamb chops
About 50g chicken livers
50g mushrooms
A dash of Worcestershire sauce
Salt and pepper
100g butter
1 egg
200g fresh breadcrumbs

METHOD

1. Preheat the oven to 190°C (375°F, Gas 5)
2. Trim some of the fat from the chops but leave about 0.5cm and make a slit through the fat and halfway through the lean section of the chop.
3. Chop the chicken livers and mushrooms and stir together in a bowl. Add a dash of Worcestershire sauce and a little salt and pepper.
4. Fry the mixture in half of the butter for a few minutes. Allow to cool.
5. Use this to stuff the opening in the chop and secure with a couple of cocktail sticks, or sew up using a darning needle and strong cotton thread.
6. Beat the egg in a dish, and dip the chops in the egg and then into the breadcrumbs.

7. Place the chops in a roasting tray. Melt the other half of the butter and pour over each of the chops.
8. Cook for 8 minutes then turn over carefully and cook for a further 8–15 minutes depending on how well done you like your meat.
9. Remove the cocktail sticks or stitches before serving.

These are delicious served with boiled potatoes and savoy cabbage.

Richmond Maids of Honour

These wonderfully satisfying little cakes were given their name by Henry Vlll who found some court ladies sitting eating them in the gardens of Hampton Court. As the ladies were maids of honour, the King tasted one and christened them Maids of Honour. Two hundred years later the recipe was handed over to a shopkeeper in Richmond-on-Thames. They are very easy to make and are very similar to curd tarts.

INGREDIENTS

Makes 14–16 cakes

200g puff pastry
220g cottage cheese
80g golden caster sugar
50g currants
Grated zest of 1 lemon
20g chopped almonds
1 egg, beaten
1 dessertspoon brandy
20g butter, melted
1 dessertspoon icing sugar for dusting

METHOD

1. Preheat the oven to 190°C (375°F, Gas 5) and grease 16 holes of 2 x 12 whole bun tins.
2. Strain all the liquid from the cottage cheese and put it in a large bowl. Chop the curds with a knife and stir in the sugar, currants, lemon zest, chopped almonds, egg, brandy and butter. Stir everything well together.
3. Roll out the pastry quite thinly and cut into circles that fit the tin holes. Make sure the pastry comes

high up the sides of the tin.
4. Spoon the cheese mixture into the pastry cases until two-thirds full.
5. Bake for 20–25 minutes until the pastry and the top is golden brown.
6. When cool, dust with icing sugar.

Tonbridge Biscuits

Crispy little biscuits topped with caraway seeds.

INGREDIENTS

Makes 8–14 biscuits depending on size and shape of cutter used.

220g plain flour
110g butter
110g caster sugar
1 egg, beaten
1 egg white
15g caraway seeds

METHOD

1. Preheat the oven to 180°C (350°F, Gas 4) and grease 2 baking sheets.
2. Sift the flour into a bowl and add the butter.
3. Rub the butter into the flour until the mixture looks like fine breadcrumbs.
4. Stir in the sugar.
5. Add the beaten egg and stir in well. Use your hands to bring the mixture to a smooth dough.
6. Roll the dough out until it is about 1cm thick, then cut out rounds with a biscuit cutter (any shape or size will do).
7. Place the biscuits on the baking sheet and brush the tops with the egg white. Sprinkle the seeds evenly over the top.
8. Bake for 10–12 minutes or until they are light golden in colour.

Honeycomb

INGREDIENTS

150ml cold water
1 tbsp golden syrup
220g golden granulated sugar
½ tsp cream of tartar
½ tsp bicarbonate of soda
1 tsp hot water

METHOD

1. Butter an 18cm square tin. Put the cold water, golden syrup, sugar and cream of tartar into a heavy-based pan on a low heat. Stir with a wooden spoon until all the sugar has dissolved.
2. Turn up the heat and bring the mixture to the boil. Don't stir at this stage.
3. Continue to boil until the mixture reaches 154°C (310°F).
4. The next step has to be done very quickly. When the toffee has reached the correct temperature remove from the heat. Mix the bicarbonate of soda with the hot water and immediately add it to the toffee mixture, stirring gently. It is fun to watch it fizz and rise!
5. Pour into the prepared tin and allow to cool and set.
6. Cut the honeycomb up as best you can – regular shapes are almost impossible as it cracks and breaks. Eat within 24 hours.

Dr Johnson's Punch

This is a hearty, winter-warming drink ideal for parties and get-togethers. This drink is supposedly a recipe made by Dr Johnson when he was entertaining his guests.

It should be drunk hot or at least warm.

INGREDIENTS

Makes about 25 servings

1 large orange
2 litres of red wine (claret or burgundy is best)
8 level tbsp caster sugar
7 whole cloves
7 whole allspice
2cm piece of fresh ginger
1.5 litres boiling water
180ml brandy
180ml Cointreau

METHOD

1. Prick the orange all over with a knife or skewer and place in a 4.5–5 litre pan.
2. Pour over the wine and stir in the sugar and spices.
3. Add the boiling water and bring to simmering point, and allow the whole thing to simmer for 30 minutes.
4. Remove the pan from the heat and add the brandy and Cointreau, stir well. Serve in punch glasses.

Chapter 2

The Midlands and the East

This expansive and varied landscape of Britain has a great industrial past but also has a rich agriculture with some of the best reared beef in the country, fruit laden orchards and natural water springs.

From Melton Mowbray pork pies to Tamworth pork, sweet sticky gingerbread to treacly Staffordshire fruitcakes. The wealth of food is as varied as the landscape.

Probably the British Midlands is responsible for one of the major food movements of the world - the Balti curry, consumed from aluminium foil tins the world over.

Jugged Hare

Use a large lidded heatproof jug or other container for this, so long as it has a well-fitting lid. If you don't have one use a large pudding basin and cover with 2 layers of greaseproof paper and a layer of foil. Tie it securely with string. You will also need a large pan to hold the jug or basin as the jugged hare is cooked inside the jug in simmering water. Your butcher will joint the hare for you.

Traditionally the dish was thickened with the blood of the hare. If you wish to do this ask the butcher to keep the blood for you, if you haven't prepared it yourself. Rather than using the kneaded butter to thicken, stir in the blood but do not allow to boil, keep the sauce just at simmering before pouring over the hare.

INGREDIENTS

Serves 4-6

1 hare, jointed
A little salt and pepper to taste
200g streaky bacon, rind removed and chopped
2 onions, chopped
150ml red wine
200ml stock or water
Juice of 1 orange
½ tsp dried marjoram
1 tsp dried parsley
A good pinch of mace
A good pinch of nutmeg
Grated zest of ½ lemon
1 tbsp. plain flour kneaded into 20g butter

METHOD

1. Season the joints of hare and place in the jug or basin it will be cooked in.

2. Put all the other ingredients except the butter and flour mixture in a bowl and mix well together. Pour this over the hare and put on the lid or secure the top of the basin.

3. Place the jug or basin in a pan and pour boiling water into the pan until it reaches about two thirds up the sides of the jug. Simmer on a low heat for 4 hours, always keeping the level of water topped up.

4. After the cooking time. Place the pieces of hare in a warm serving dish and keep warm.

5. Pour all the juices from the container into a saucepan and add the flour and butter mixture, whisk as it reaches boiling point, then simmer for 3 minutes before pouring over the hare.

Shropshire Pea Soup

Not the thick heavy dried pea soup that is welcome in the autumn or winter months but a fresher summer one that uses either freshly podded or frozen peas.

INGREDIENTS

Serves 4-6

25g butter
1 onion, chopped finely
650g freshly podded peas or frozen ones
1.2 litres vegetable stock
½ teaspoon caster sugar
About 8 fresh mint leaves, chopped
Salt and pepper to taste
2 egg yolks
150ml double cream
Sprigs of mint to garnish

METHOD

1. Melt the butter in a saucepan and fry the onion gently until soft.
2. Add the peas and cook with onions for a further 3 minutes, stirring gently.
3. Add the stock, sugar, mint and any seasoning necessary. Bring to the boil then simmer on a medium heat for 15 minutes.
4. Blend the soup to your taste or pass through a sieve. Then return to the pan and beat in the egg and stir in the cream.
5. Heat gently until the soup thickens and serve.

Potted Stilton

This is very easy and quick to prepare and makes and excellent buffet party dish or for snacks served with crackers or crusty bread.

INGREDIENTS

250g Stilton, blue or white
50g unsalted butter at room temperature, don't use salted as the cheese is salty enough
Pinch of mace or nutmeg
½ teaspoon English mustard

METHOD

1. Put the cheese in a bowl with all the other ingredients and mash well together with a fork.
2. Spoon into ramekins and serve at room temperature.
3. If you wish to make this to serve at a later date, melt some butter and pour a thin layer over the top of the cheese mixture to seal.

Birmingham Chicken Balti

Birmingham is famous for its balti triangle, the dish becoming popular in the 1970's. It is a fast cooking curry so needs a high temperature and a sturdy pan to prepare it.

INGREDIENTS

Serves 2

1 teaspoon garam masala
2 dried curry leaves, crushed
1 teaspoons each ground cumin, coriander cinnamon, cloves and turmeric
½ teaspoon mustard seeds
1 teaspoon soft brown sugar
½ teaspoon salt
2-3 green chilies, chopped
3 cardamom pods, crushed to release the seeds
2 tablespoons vegetable oil
1 onion, chopped
2 cloves garlic, chopped
1cm piece of fresh ginger root, grated
2 chicken breasts, diced
300ml stock
1 tablespoon tomato puree
1-2 tablespoons freshly chopped coriander leaves

METHOD

1. Mix together the spices, chilies, sugar and salt in a small dish.
2. Heat the oil in a large pan and add the onions and garlic, fry for a few minutes then stir in the ginger root and mixed spices.
3. Add the chicken breast and cook for 4-5 minutes

stirring constantly, turn down the heat as it is cooking if necessary.

4. Stir in the stock and tomato puree and simmer for 20 minutes.

5. Add the fresh coriander just before removing from the heat and serving with boiled basmati rice and/or warm naan.

Roast Rib of Hereford Beef with Horseradish Cream

A family favourite from all over England, but try it with this very special cut of beef from the Midlands for a celebration meal.

INGREDIENTS

Serves 8

Rib of beef joint weighing approximately 3 kg
Salt and pepper to taste

For the horseradish cream:
75g horseradish, grated finely
250ml single cream
2 tablespoon soured cream or crème fraiche
1 tablespoon white wine vinegar
2 teaspoons caster sugar

METHOD
1. Preheat the oven to 220ºC (430ºF, gas mark 7).
2. Pat the joint dry with kitchen paper and place in a large roasting tin.
3. Season to taste all over the upper surface of the joint.
4. Pour sufficient hot water in the base of the pan to about 1cm.
5. Place in the hot oven for about 30 minutes until the fat is browned then turn the oven down to 170ºC (340ºF, gas mark 3) and cook for:
   a. 10 minutes per 500g + 10 minutes for rare
   b. 15 minutes per 500g + 15 minutes for medium

      c. 20 minutes per 500g + 20 minutes for well
          done

6.   When cooked to your taste leave the meat to rest
        for 30 minutes before serving.

For the horseradish cream:
Put all the ingredients in a bowl and mix thoroughly together.
Serve with the roast beef.

Fidget Pie

A harvest time favourite traditionally made as a welcoming supper after a long day in the fields for farm workers.

INGREDIENTS

Serves 4-6

3 large potatoes, peeled and thinly sliced
400g gammon, sliced in small thin pieces
2 medium onions, sliced thinly
3 cooking apples, cored, peeled and sliced
1 tablespoon sugar, sprinkle this over the apple slices
½ teaspoon dried thyme
250-300ml stock
250g shortcrust pastry

METHOD

1. Preheat the oven to 180ºC (350ºF, gas mark 4) and butter a deep pie dish.
2. Alternately layer the filling thus, potato, gammon, onion and apple, repeating until the dish is full.
3. Stir the thyme into the stock and pour sufficient liquid over the filling to just cover.
4. Roll out the pastry to fit the top of the pie and place firmly on the filling.
5. Bake for an hour.
6. Serve hot with a green vegetable and extra buttered boiled potatoes.

Tamworth Pork Chops with Mushroom Pâté

You can prepare this recipe with any type of pork but if you can source Tamworth pork it is well worth while.

INGREDIENTS

Serves 4

2 tablespoons oil
4 Tamworth pork chops
20g butter
1 small onion or 2 shallots, chopped finely
1 garlic clove, grated or crushed
100g mushrooms, chopped finely
About 50g breadcrumbs
Salt and pepper to taste
Sufficient cream cheese to smear each chop thickly.

METHOD

1. Preheat the oven to 190ºC (370ºF, gas mark 5).
2. Fry the pork chops in the oil to just seal the meat and lightly brown. Place in a lightly oiled roasting tin.
3. Melt the butter in the same pan and fry the onion or shallots gently until translucent.
4. Add the garlic and mushrooms then fry until cooked. Season to taste.
5. Remove from the heat and stir in sufficient breadcrumbs to soak up the juices.
6. Spread cream cheese over the upper surface of the chops and spoon equal amounts of the mushroom mixture over the top, pressing it into the cheese.
7. Cover the pan with foil and cook for about 20-25,

remove the foil after 15 minutes.

8. Serve with a salad or boiled new potatoes and a green vegetable. This dish also goes well with corn on the cob.

Sticky Staffordshire Gingerbread

This is a traditional autumn sweet treat in the region. Leave this to get stickier for a day or two in an airtight container.

INGREDIENTS

Makes about 14 pieces

220g self-raising flour
2 level teaspoon ground ginger
¼ teaspoon salt
100g soft brown sugar
120g butter
1 tablespoon golden syrup
2 teaspoons dark treacle
1 egg

METHOD

1. Preheat the oven to 175ºC (350ºF, gas mark 3) and grease an 18cm by 10cm rectangular tin.
2. Sift the flour ginger and salt together into a mixing bowl and stir in the sugar.
3. Melt the butter, syrup and treacle together over a low heat.
4. Remove from the heat and stir in the egg.
5. Pour the butter mixture into the flour and mix thoroughly together.
6. Spoon into the prepared tin and bake for about 30 minutes until well risen and springy to the touch.
7. Allow to cool for a few minutes then cut into pieces of whatever size you wish. Bigger pieces are easier to remove from the tin. After cooling in the tin for about 20 minutes, transfer to a cooling rack.
8. Store in a lidded container. The gingerbread will get

stickier if left for a day.
9. For a glossy top brush with warm syrup, honey or apricot jam.

Chapter 3

Wonderful Wales

Wales is our second home – our children grew up with Anglesey and North Wales holidays. We visit Wales every other week for various reasons and have found a wonderful pub that sells the best food we have ever tasted. It is simple, fresh and cooked whilst you wait. Lamb and mixed grills, fish and Welsh pies are all on the menu. But my favourite is beer-battered fish, chips and mushy peas.

There are many signature dishes from Wales, none more famous than their Bara brith. This first soup recipe uses leeks which are one of my favourite vegetables. It is also very simple to prepare and makes an excellent winter warmer on a chilly day.

Cawl Cennin/Cream of Leek Soup

Serve with some crusty bread or even a bacon sandwich.

INGREDIENTS

Serves 6

600g leeks, washed, trimmed and sliced thinly
2 sticks celery with the leaves still attached, washed and chopped finely
2 medium-sized potatoes, peeled and diced
30g butter
1 litre vegetable stock
1 tbsp fresh chopped parsley
2 sprigs thyme
300ml milk
200ml double cream
Salt and pepper
A pinch nutmeg

METHOD

1. Melt the butter in a large lidded pan and add the leeks and celery. Cover and allow to sweat on a low light for 10 minutes. Lift out a couple of pieces of leek to garnish the soup just before serving.
2. Add the potatoes and herbs and stir well, cook for 5 minutes.
3. Add the stock and bring to the boil. Then cover and simmer for 10 minutes.
4. Stir in the milk, and salt and pepper to taste. Simmer for 5 minutes.
5. Stir in the cream and serve whilst hot with a garnish of the reserved leeks.

Some recipes call for a small onion to be added but I have tried it with and without and prefer just the leek flavour. But if you wish to add an onion, chop it finely and add to the leeks at the beginning of the cooking time.

Caws Pob/Welsh Rarebit

This is a favourite toast topper. It is a traditional recipe that an aunt used to make for us when we visited her beautiful cottage on the edge of the beach at Criccieth.

INGREDIENTS

Serves 2

20g butter
20g plain flour
1 tsp Dijon mustard
A dash of Worcestershire sauce
50ml porter beer or dark ale
200–250g grated cheddar cheese
4 slices of bread
Black pepper to taste

METHOD

1. Preheat the grill.
2. Melt the butter, mustard and Worcestershire sauce together over a low heat and add the flour, stir well to combine.
3. Gradually add the beer to make a thick sauce. Season with black pepper.
4. Stir in the cheese.
5. Toast the bread lightly and spread one side with the cheese mixture.
6. Grill until the top is brown and serve immediately.

Pâté Gregyn Gleision y Fenai/Menai Strait Mussel Pâté

This makes a wonderful starter or snack dish. A seafood lover's dream. You don't have to use Menai mussels but you really should visit, it is a most glorious stretch of water.

INGREDIENTS

Serves 2 – 3

150g cooked mussels (shelled weight), chopped finely or minced in a food processor
50g grated carrot
20g grated celery
30g fresh breadcrumbs
2 eggs, beaten
50g herring roe
1 tbsp. fresh chopped mixed herbs, parsley, dill, thyme and tarragon or any combination of more than one of the four
1 clove garlic
1 tbsp. brandy
1 tbsp. cream

METHOD

1. Preheat the oven to 170°C (340°F, gas mark 3) and butter a loaf or terrine tin.
2. Put all the ingredients into a bowl and combine them with your hands – it is the only way to ensure a good mix.
3. Press the mixture into the loaf or terrine tin. Pack it down well.
4. Put the tin into a roasting tin and pour in sufficient water to reach half way up the tin.

5. Cook for 30–40 minutes until the pâté is firm to the touch.

6. Serve with hot buttered toast.

Tatws Popty/Oven-Baked Potatoes

This is a great accompaniment to cooked meats and a change from mashed potatoes when served with sausages.

INGREDIENTS

Serves 6 as an accompaniment

4 large or 6 medium potatoes, peeled and sliced thickly
50g butter
1 tbsp flour seasoned with ½ tsp salt and pepper
2 onions, sliced thickly
200ml water
200ml milk
Salt and pepper to taste

METHOD

1. Spread half of the butter into an ovenproof dish or roasting pan and preheat the oven to 180°C (350°F, gas mark 4).
2. Put half of the potatoes in a layer into the dish, overlapping each slice.
3. Sprinkle over the seasoned flour evenly.
4. Add the onions as a layer over the potatoes.
5. Put in the rest of the potatoes, layered over the top of the onions. Dot with the rest of the butter.
6. Mix the milk and water and pour over the potatoes and onions.
7. Cover with foil and bake in the oven for 1 ½ hours. Remove the foil and bake for 20 more minutes uncovered.

8. Serve with roasted meats or grilled sausages.

Casserol Ceredigion/Cardiganshire Casserole

INGREDIENTS

Serves 4

450g potatoes, peeled and sliced thickly
1 onion, sliced
1 tbsps. oil
500g minced beef
200g tomatoes, chopped
½ tsp curry powder
½ tsp sage
250ml vegetable or beef stock

For the sauce topping:
300ml natural yoghurt
2 eggs
50g flour
½ tsp dry mustard powder
100g Welsh cheese (any will do)
Salt and pepper to taste

METHOD

1. Preheat the oven to 180°C (350°F, gas mark 4).
2. Boil the potatoes until just tender then leave to drain and cool.
3. Heat the oil in a frying pan and fry the onions until soft then add the meat and fry them together until the meat changes colour.
4. Stir in the tomatoes, curry powder and sage and simmer for 4 minutes.
5. Pour in the stock and simmer for 15 minutes.

6. Put the mixture into an ovenproof dish.
7. Layer the potatoes on the top, overlapping them and cook in the oven for 30 minutes.
8. Make the sauce by beating the eggs and yoghurt together.
9. Beat in the flour and mustard powder.
10. Stir in the cheese and season with salt and pepper to taste.
11. Lift the casserole out of the oven and pour the yoghurt mixture over the top.
12. Return to the oven and bake for a further 25–30 minutes until the top is brown.

Serve with glazed carrots and or peas.

Wyau Ynys Mon/Anglesey Eggs

A very tasty supper dish that is very economical to make.

INGREDIENTS

Serves 4–6

6 small leeks, sliced
300ml milk
A knob of butter
450g mashed potato
8 boiled eggs, shelled
100g grated cheddar
1 tbsp flour
25g butter
2–3 tbsp breadcrumbs
Salt and pepper
A little grated nutmeg

METHOD

1. Poach the leeks in the milk with a knob of butter for about 10 minutes or until tender.
2. Drain the leeks and reserve the poaching liquid.
3. Mix the mashed potato and leeks. Spoon the mash and leek mixture into an ovenproof dish. Preheat the oven to 180°C (350°F, gas mark 4).
4. Make a cheese sauce by melting the butter in a pan over a low heat and stirring in the flour.
5. Gradually add the poaching liquid and a little more milk if the sauce is too thick.
6. Bring the sauce to the boil, stirring all the time. Turn down the heat and simmer for 2 minutes.
7. Remove from the heat and stir in the cheese, reserving a small handful for the top, and season

with any extra salt and pepper to taste.

8. Halve the eggs lengthways and place them on top of the potato and leek mixture.

9. Pour over the cheese sauce and sprinkle the top with the breadcrumbs and the rest of the cheese. Finish with a little nutmeg.

10. Bake for 20 minutes or until the mixture is bubbling and the top is golden brown.

Pwdin Mynwy/Monmouth Pudding

The base mixture of this is very similar to the queen of puddings as it combines breadcrumbs, eggs and milk with a jam filling and topping.

INGREDIENTS

Serves 4

450ml milk
30g butter
30g golden caster sugar
The grated zest of 1 lemon
180g fresh breadcrumbs
2 eggs
5 tbsps. strawberry or raspberry jam

METHOD

1. Put the milk in a saucepan over a low heat and stir in the sugar, butter and lemon zest.
2. Bring to the boil, stirring constantly.
3. Remove from the heat and stir in the breadcrumbs.
4. Leave to cool, and when ready beat in the eggs. Preheat the oven to 190°C (375°F, gas mark 5) and butter a pudding dish or basin.
5. Spoon half of the milk and egg mixture into the basin.
6. Melt the jam in a pan and pour half over the pudding mixture.
7. Spoon the rest of the pudding mixture over the jam and top with the rest of the jam.
8. Bake for 35–40 minutes or until the pudding has set.

I like to serve this with some cream.

Bara Brith Pentref/Village Bara Brith

This is a very easy version of bara brith. It is very economical and tastes better if you allow it to mature for a day before slicing.

INGREDIENTS

280g dried mixed fruit
150g soft brown sugar
450ml cold tea
350g self-raising flour
1 tsp mixed spice
1 tsp baking powder
2 eggs, beaten

METHOD

1. Put the fruit and sugar together in a large mixing bowl. Combine well with a wooden spoon and pour over the cold tea. Leave to soak overnight.
2. Preheat the oven to 150°C (300°F, gas mark 2) and butter a 1kg loaf tin.
3. Sift the flour, spice and baking powder together into the fruit mixture and stir well.
4. Beat in the eggs.
5. Pour the mixture into the prepared loaf tin and bake for 1 ½ hours.
6. Allow to cool in the tin for 15 minutes then transfer to a cooling rack. When completely cool, wrap in greaseproof paper and store in an airtight container.

This is wonderful sliced and spread with butter.

Cacenau Aberhonddu/Brecon Light Cakes

These are delightful little cakes or pancakes and the hint of orange gives a tangy flavour.

INGREDIENTS

Makes about 8 cakes

2 eggs
2 tbsp orange juice
25g golden caster sugar
3 tbsp milk
120g self-raising flour
About 25g butter for frying, a little more if you are doing them in several batches
30g demerara sugar

METHOD

1. Beat the eggs and orange juice together.
2. Sift the flour into a mixing bowl and stir in the sugar.
3. Stir the milk into the egg mixture and pour into the flour.
4. Mix well with a wooden spoon and set aside for 5 minutes.
5. Melt the butter in a large frying pan and drop a tablespoon of the batter into the pan and cook on both sides for 2–3 minutes or until golden brown. Cook all the batter in this way and when they are cooked sprinkle with brown sugar.

Serve when cool.

Loshin Du/Black Toffee

This is delicious Welsh treacle toffee.

INGREDIENTS

Makes about 800g

120g butter
450g granulated sugar
2 tbsp warm water
2 tbsp white vinegar
4 tbsp black treacle

METHOD

1. Melt the butter in a sturdy pan and stir in the sugar and treacle.
2. Add the vinegar and water and stir well until the sugar has dissolved.
3. Bring to boiling point, then boil steadily for 15 minutes or until a little of the toffee snaps when it is put into a bowl of cold water. Use a preserving thermometer if you wish – the temperature should reach 152°C/305°F.
4. Pour the toffee into a buttered rectangular tin that measures about 28cm by 18cm.
5. Leave to cool for 30 minutes then score it into squares.
6. When cold, break up the squares and wrap in cellophane or baking paper.

Store in an airtight container.

Chapter 4

The South West

Cornwall is a place of which I know very little, but many of my friends and family holiday there regularly. Devon I know, especially wonderful Dartmouth and Kingswear. On our travels down to Dartmouth we would always look out for 'The Willow Man' striking a pose in a field celebrating Somerset's apple harvest.

One of the archetypal foods of the region are apples and pears. These crops simply pervade much of the food, and of course drink, of the region.

The food of the region is for people who work the land and mine the lead so consequently is wholesome and filling. But there are some dainties to be had, and probably the very best cheese in the world!

Salcombe Bay Crab Soup

A luxurious soup that makes an excellent dinner party course or just as a treat. If fresh crab is unavailable then simply use frozen. Don't forget to use the shells for making the stock, if you have them.

INGREDIENTS

Serves 4-6

25g butter
1 onion, chopped finely
1 stick celery, chopped
80g long grain rice
650ml fish stock
300ml milk
100ml dry white wine
About 250g crab meat
2 tsp anchovy essence
Good pinch cayenne pepper
150ml double cream
1 tbsps. fresh chopped parsley
Salt and pepper to taste

METHOD

1. Melt the butter in a saucepan and fry the onion and celery together over a lowish heat without browning until soft.
2. Add the rice, stock, milk and wine and bring to the boil. Reduce the heat and simmer until the rice is cooked, about 15 minutes.
3. Add the crab meat, anchovy essence and season with the cayenne, salt and pepper. Cook gently for 3 minutes stirring to mix the ingredients.
4. Add the cream and parsley and warm through.

5. Serve immediately with a little parsley to garnish and thin melba toast.

Cornish Pasties

A hefty pasty to satisfy the Cornish miners appetite makes an all-in-one meal for anyone, served with pickles or your favourite chutney.

INGREDIENTS

Makes 4 large pasties.

500g short crust pastry
1 onion, finely chopped
400g best braising steak cut into very small chunks
3 medium sized potatoes, sliced into thin crisp-like strips rather than diced
120g diced swede
50g butter
Salt and plenty of white pepper
1 egg yolk mixed with 4 tbsps. milk

METHOD

1. Preheat the oven to 200ºC (390ºF, gas mark 6).
2. Cut the pastry into 4 equal portions and roll each one to about the size of a small dinner plate.
3. In a bowl combine the vegetables and place a quarter of the mixture in the centre of the pastry circles.
4. Season with salt and pepper.
5. Place a quarter of the meat in the centre of the vegetables and season a little more over the meat.
6. Dot the filling with butter.
7. Dampen the edges and fold to make a semi-circle. Turn the edges over to seal and crimp with finger and thumb.

8. Place each pasty on a greased baking sheet and brush with the egg and milk mixture.
9. Bake for 15 minutes then turn down the heat to180ºC (360ºF, gas mark 4) and bake for about 40 minutes. Turn the heat down to 170ºC (350ºF, gas mark 3) after 30 minutes if the pastry is cooking too quickly.

Gloucester Cheese and Ale

This is a quick and warming dish of cheese served with mustard and ale.

INGREDIENTS

Serves 2

150g Double Gloucester Cheese, grated
1 level tsp English mustard
100ml-150ml strong ale
4 thick slices of toasted buttered bread

METHOD
1. Put the cheese in a bowl with the mustard and mix well, then transfer to an oven proof dish.
2. Pour over sufficient ale to just cover the cheese mixture.
3. Place under a hot grill until the cheese melts then pour over the toast.
4. Add more or less mustard to your taste.

Somerset Pork

Wonderful apple and pork combination makes this one of our favourites.

INGREDIENTS

Serves 4

30g butter or 2 tbsp. oil
4 good sized pork chops
1 onion, sliced
2 cloves garlic, chopped
2 large dessert apples, cored and sliced thinly, peel if you prefer
250ml dry cider
150ml double cream
Salt and pepper

METHOD
1. Preheat the oven to 190ºC (370ºF, gas mark 5).
2. Heat the oil or butter in a frying pan and seal the chops all over. Transfer to a casserole dish.
3. Fry the onions in the same pan until soft and add to the meat.
4. Fry the apple slices in the same pan allowing to colour slightly. Arrange over the meat and onions. Season with salt and pepper to taste.
5. Pour the cider into the same pan stirring to deglaze the pan. Bring to the boil and then pour over the meat.
6. Cover and cook for about 35-40 minutes or until the meat is tender.
7. Stir in the cream and cover and cook for 5 more minutes to heat through.

I like to serve this with baked jacket potatoes and some green vegetables.

Liver Casserole

The combination of lambs liver and good quality bacon is delicious.
This dish was sent to me by a friend who lives in West Somerset. It was his Grandma's recipe.
The majority of recipes in this book have been passed down, found in notebooks kept by grandmothers and not thrown away.

INGREDIENTS

Serves 4

2 tbsp. oil
8 rashers bacon, cut into pieces
2 medium onions, chopped
400g lambs liver, sliced
1 tbsp. seasoned flour
2 medium carrots sliced into discs
50g mushrooms, sliced if large
450ml beef or vegetable stock
Dash of Worcestershire sauce
Salt and pepper

METHOD
1. Preheat the oven to 180ºC (360ºF, gas mark 4).
2. Fry the bacon in the oil adding the onions after a few minutes. Fry for 3 minutes.
3. Coat the pieces of liver in the seasoned flour and fry with the bacon gently. Place in a casserole dish.
4. Add the carrots and mushrooms.
5. Deglaze the pan with the stock and pour over the meat and vegetables, stirring to combine.
6. Add the Worcestershire sauce and salt and pepper to taste. Remember, the flour was seasoned, so

don't over season at this point. It is always best to under season because you can always add more later.

7. Cover and cook in the oven for 45-50 minutes.

Serve with boiled potatoes and extra vegetables if you wish.

Dorset Apple Cake

A traditional cake that is good served sliced with tea or as a dessert with cream.

INGREDIENTS

250g cooking apples peeled, cored, sliced and sprinkled with lemon juice
250g self raising flour
1 tsp ground cinnamon
150g butter, cut into small pieces
150g soft brown sugar
2 eggs
4 tbsp. milk
A tablespoon of Demerara sugar mixed with a pinch of ground cinnamon

METHOD
1. Grease and line an 18cm deep round cake tin and preheat the oven to 180ºC (360ºF, gas mark 4).
2. Sift the flour and cinnamon into a mixing bowl.
3. Rub in the butter.
4. Stir in the sugar.
5. Mix in the egg and milk well beating with a wooden spoon.
6. Stir in the apples.
7. Spoon into the prepared tin and sprinkle over the sugar and cinnamon mixture.
8. Bake for about 50 minutes until cooked in the centre. Use a fine skewer to test. If it comes away clean it is cooked.

Roasted Belly Pork

Long slow cooking for a delicious finish to this meat.

Ingredients

Serves 4

About 1kg joint of belly pork
3 cloves of garlic cut into slices
Salt and pepper

1. Preheat the oven to 160C/gas mark 2
2. Place the joint skin side down on a clean work surface and season with salt and pepper lightly.
3. Place the slice of garlic evenly over the meat
4. Take a large piece of foil big enough to cover the meat and down the sides but leaving the skin free of foil. Press the foil snugly around the meat and carefully lift the whole thing up and place a roasting pan with the skin open on the top and the foil is underneath the meat.
5. Salt the top part of the skin lightly to help it crisp up.
6. Place in the oven and roast for 30 minutes at 160C/gas mark 2 then turn the heat down to 150C/gas mark 1 and roast for 2 ½ hours.

To vary:

Add a sprinkling of rosemary or a pinch of sage with the garlic
Brush the skin with a good coating of honey before seasoning for a sticky crackling.

Stargazy Pie

This pie is one of those traditional dishes that many people have heard of, but unless you live in Cornwall have probably never tasted. It was originally from the coastal Cornish village of Mousehole, where the main occupation has been fishing for many years.

The pie is unlike any other fish based pie as it has the fishes heads poking out from the pastry crust, hence the name 'Stargazy'.

The pie is traditionally eaten in Cornwall on 23rd December, Tom Bawcock's Eve.

It is to celebrate the legendary character Tom who is supposed to have saved Mousehole from starvation during a period of very bad storms. None of the locals could go out on their usual fishing trips because of the weather so there was no food around.

But Tom Bawcock risked his life and took to the seas and fished for as big a catch as he could. When he returned with his haul back to shore they made a huge fish pie. It contained so many fish that their heads began to protrude from the crust and this story is remembered in the making of 'Stargazy Pie'.

The celebrations include a wonderful display of lanterns in many different shapes usually based around Christmas symbols, reindeer, Santa, Christmas trees and the like. The villagers make a huge Stargazy pie that is lit up with many candles.

The whole festival is a spectacle par excellence and one that I have only seen on the television but would love to be a part of one day. If any of our readers have been at this wonderful festival please let us know!

There are many actual recipes for this dish. Though all have the traditional heads of some fish or other poking out of the pastry lid, it is the rest of the ingredients that can be slightly different. The first recipe is one that uses only pilchards, or sardines if you cannot get pilchards, and is the most traditional of the recipes.

Cornish Stargazy Pie

Ingredients

Serves 4 -6

12 large sardines or 8 pilchards
1 large onion, chopped finely
1 tablespoon fresh, chopped parsley
8 rashers of streaky bacon, chopped
3 eggs, softly boiled
Juice of 1 lemon
Milk to glaze
450g/1lb pack ready-made short crust pastry (or make your own if you wish)
Salt and pepper to taste

METHOD

1. Clean and bone the fish and season the insides. Remove the heads of all but 3 of the pilchards or 4 of the sardines.
2. Combine the bacon, eggs, onion and parsley in a bowl.
3. Grease a large pie dish and roll out a thin disc of half of the pastry to fit the dish and line the dish with the pastry.
4. Put a little of the bacon mixture inside each of the fish and place the headless fish on the pastry in a circle, tails in the centre and pile the rest of the bacon mixture over and around the fish.
5. Pour the lemon juice over the fish and season to taste.
6. Roll out the other half of the pastry and wet the edges of the pie before placing the lid on top of the

fish.

7. Make a slit in the pastry big enough to contain a head and place each fish head in a pastry slit.
8. Glaze the top of the pie with milk and bake for 40 minutes at 180c/gas 4 until the pie is golden in colour.

You could also leave the heads on all the fish and lay them in the pie with their heads poking out round the outer edge of the pie, so when you place the top crust on the dish tuck the pastry well down between the fish. This stops you from having to place them through slits in the top crust and everyone gets a head!

Luxury Stargazy Pie

This still has the wow effect of the traditional pie but has a more luxurious flavour and can be served as a dinner party main course with some new potatoes and a green salad.

INGREDIENTS

Serves 4

3 pilchards
6 sardines
100g/4oz salmon fillet
100g/4oz peeled large prawns
100g/4oz cod or haddock or similar white fish
Small wine glass of white wine
6 tablespoons double cream
2 hard boiled eggs
1 tablespoon fresh chopped parsley
Salt and pepper to taste
225g/8oz shortcrust pastry

METHOD

1. Butter a deep pie dish. Prepare the sardines and pilchards as before, reserving the heads of the pilchards.
2. Cut the salmon and white fish into large chunks and place in the pie dish with the sardines, prawns, chopped hardboiled eggs and sprinkle parsley over the fish. Season with salt and pepper.
3. Whisk the wine into the cream and pour over the fish.
4. Roll out the pastry to cover the dish and hang over the edge slightly. Make 3 slits in the top of the pastry and place the heads of the pilchards in the slits

looking up to the skies as before.

5. Glaze the pie with a little milk and bake for 40-45 minutes at 180C/gas 4 until pastry is golden brown.

6. If you like the sauce in the pie thicker, combine a little of the wine with a teaspoon of cornflour and whisk into the cream mixture before pouring over the fish.

COOKING BRITAIN

Chapter 5

The North West

This area is our families birth place and we are obviously very proud of it. It is a beautiful place full of mountains, rolling hills, lakes and some of the most productive coastlines for sea food. The traditional ingredients have suddenly become very fashionable for top class chefs to use in their dishes. Black pudding seems to be on every restaurants menu, as is Lancashire hot Pot.

Our family heralds from Southport, so I spent many a happy day trying to find the sea on Ainsdale beach. On our way home we would call in to a local Ormskirk farmer we knew and stock up on fresh vegetables. The potatoes were dug up by my dad and brother and we would have fried eggs and freshly made chips with the potatoes, simple but glorious. In summer we would go into Cheshire and pick our own strawberries and raspberries for eating fresh or jam and pie making.

Potted Shrimp or Prawns

The Lancashire coast is famous for its seafood and potted brown shrimps make a simple yet tasty starter course or quick lunch dish. Add more or less cayenne pepper to taste.

INGREDIENTS

Serves 2

250g brown shrimp or prawns
80g melted butter
¼ teaspoon cayenne pepper
A little salt
Black pepper

METHOD
1. Force as many prawns or shrimp as will fit into ramekin dishes and season with salt and black pepper.
2. Whilst the butter is melting add the cayenne pepper and stir to mix thoroughly. Pour the butter over the shrimp or prawns and allow to set before serving with hot toast. The butter from the prawns will melt into your toast. Delicious!

Try topping a piece of poached or fried hake with spoonful of potted prawns, the butter melts into the fish, a wonderful yet easy special meal.

Seafood Soup

This is a seafood lovers dish. Morecombe Bay has the ideal ingredients for this recipe.

INGREDIENTS

Serves 4 as a main course or 6 as a starter

600ml fish stock or water
200g haddock
200g whiting or other white fish
250g cooked peeled prawns, defrosted if frozen
100g mussels
50g cockles
1 medium sized onion, chopped finely
2 cloves garlic, chopped
1 tablespoon butter
1 tablespoon plain flour
600ml milk
Pinch grated nutmeg
2 tablespoons lemon juice
½ small glass dry white wine
4 tablespoons single cream
1 tablespoon of freshly chopped parsley
Salt and black pepper

METHOD

1. Poach the haddock and other white fish in the milk for 5 minutes with some salt, black pepper and the nutmeg.
2. Strain the fish, retaining the milk. Flake the fish and check for any bones.
3. In a large pan melt the butter and fry the onion gently without browning until they are soft. Add the

garlic and stir.

4. Remove from the heat and stir in the flour. Place back on the heat and gradually add the poaching milk and the stock or water, stirring with a wooden spoon until all the liquid is combined with the flour mixture.

5. Add the lemon juice and wine, stirring in vigorously. Raise the heat to bring the soup to boiling point. Once boiled, turn down to a low simmer. Test for seasoning.

6. Add the flaked fish, prawns, mussels, cockles and half of the parsley. Simmer for 5 minutes. Stir in the cream and serve garnished with the rest of the parsley.

Cumbrian Farmyard Cakes

These are more like food towers than cakes. We stayed in an exceptional B&B just outside Kendal and had these for breakfast.

INGREDIENTS
Serves 3 or 6 depending on how hungry you are.

500g Cumberland sausage
6 slices of bread, cut into rounds
6 eggs
Oil for frying

METHOD

1. Remove the meat from the sausage skins and form into 6 round patties approximately the same size as the bread.
2. Fry the patties until they are cooked on both sides. Keep warm.
3. Fry the bread in a little oil until golden and crispy and poach the eggs.
4. Serve a slice of bread with a sausage patty on top and finish with a poached egg.

Black Pudding, Lancashire Cheese and Walnut Salad

Here is a different way to serve black pudding. It is a tasty salad that is suitable for lunch or as a starter course.

INGREDIENTS

Serves 4

2 tbsp oil
250g smoked bacon, cut into small chunks
150g black pudding, cut into cubes
50g walnuts
150g Lancashire cheese, cubed
100g mixed salad leaves

For the dressing:
2 tbsp virgin olive oil
2 tbsp cider vinegar
1 tsp chopped fresh dill

METHOD
1. Heat the oil in a frying pan and fry the bacon and black pudding until crisp.
2. Meanwhile arrange the leaves on plates.
3. Share the walnuts and cheese between the different plates and spoon over the bacon and black pudding mixture.
4. Whisk the dressing ingredients together and drizzle over the salad.

Serve immediately.

Meat and Potato Hash with Onions in Vinegar

This is one of my Mums recipes that she would make on a cold winter's day. The smell of it cooking when I came home from school was so comforting and homely. It was also a traditional New Year's Eve dish to keep us dancing until the early hours of New Year's Day. We always had sliced onions in malt vinegar with it. Any leftover onions made a wonderful cheese sandwich the day after.

INGREDIENTS

Serves 4

500g stewing steak, cut into small chunks
400g onions, sliced
4 medium carrots, chopped into discs
500g potatoes, peeled and cut into chunks
Salt and white pepper to taste
500ml beef stock
1 tablespoon flour
1 tablespoon oil

METHOD

1. Heat the oil in a saucepan and fry the onions gently until they are soft.
2. Add the meat and fry until it all changes colour then pour over most of the stock leaving a couple of tablespoons to mix with the flour.
3. Stew the meat at simmering for 1 ¼ hours then add the rest of the stock with the flour and stir until it thickens. Add a bit more water if it is too thick.
4. Add the potatoes and season with salt and pepper.
5. Simmer for a further 20 mins until the potatoes are cooked.

To make the onions in vinegar:

Slice a large or 2 small onions thinly and put in a lidded jar. Season with salt and white pepper and pour over sufficient malt vinegar to just cover. Screw the lid on and give a it a shake. If you do this before cooking the meat for the hash, the onions will be ready to serve with the meal.

Lancashire Hot Pot

This was traditionally made in the bread oven and left to cook all day after the bread was made. It was usually made with mutton but this is often difficult to get hold of so use neck of lamb cut into cutlets or any cheaper cut of lamb.

INGREDIENTS

Serves 6

1.5kg lamb
50g lambs kidney, chopped
2 large onions, sliced thickly
600ml meat stock
150g mushrooms
1.2 kg potatoes, peeled and sliced thickly
30g butter
Salt and pepper

METHOD

1. Preheat the oven to 180ºC (350ºF, gas mark 4). Season the lamb with salt and pepper and put a layer of the lamb in a buttered casserole dish. Then add a layer of onions.
2. Add another layer of cutlets, mushrooms and the kidney, then some more onions and a layer of potatoes.
3. Pour over the stock.
4. Layer like this and finish with overlapped potatoes.
5. Dot with butter and cover. Place in the oven and cook for 2 hours.
6. Remove the lid and cook for another hour.

I like to serve this with peas and carrot and swede, boiled or steamed together and chopped with a little butter and plenty of white pepper.

Scouse

This is a traditional dish from Liverpool, similar to a hot pot.

INGREDIENTS

Serves 6 – 8

500g neck of lamb, cut into large cubes and the large bits of fat removed
500g stewing beef, cut into large cubes
1 tablespoon oil
3 onions, sliced thickly
450g carrots, peeled if you wish and cut into thick discs
1kg potatoes, peeled and sliced
600ml beef stock
3-4 sprigs thyme
Salt and pepper

METHOD

1. Preheat the oven to 170ºC (340ºF, gas mark 3).
2. Fry the meat in the oil to seal and transfer to a large casserole dish.
3. Fry the onions for 3-4 minutes then add them to the meat.
4. Chop up one potatoes worth of slices until they are small pieces and add them to the meat.
5. Mix in the carrot so they are evenly spread throughout the dish.
6. Add the thyme and pour over the stock.
7. Press the potatoes into the meat mixture and leave some on the top.
8. Season to taste and cover with a lid or foil. Put in the oven and cook for 4 hours.

Grasmere Gingerbread

This is a crumbly golden slice, somewhere between a cake and a biscuit.
Traditionally made for the rush-bearing ceremony in Grasmere.

INGREDIENTS

Makes 12-14 servings

220g self-raising flour
80g granulated sugar
2 level tsp ground ginger
Pinch salt
120g butter
1 tbsp golden syrup
2 egg yolks
100g mixed chopped peel

For the topping:
1 egg white
1 tbsp. caster sugar

METHOD
1. Preheat the oven to 170ºC (340ºF, gas mark 3) and grease an 18cm by 10cm rectangular tin.
2. Sift the flour, salt and ginger together into a mixing bowl and stir in the sugar.
3. Melt the butter and syrup in a pan over a low heat.
4. Beat the eggs into the butter mixture and add to the flour. Mix well with a wooden spoon.
5. Press half of the mixture into the prepared tin and press well down with the back of the spoon.
6. Sprinkle the mixed peel over the surface of the dough and top with the other half of the gingerbread

mixture. Press down well.
7. Brush the top with the egg white and sprinkle with the sugar.
8. Bake for 30 minutes.
9. Allow to cool for 5 minutes then cut into the desired amount of squares.

Manchester Tart

Of course I had to include this. Manchester tart was my school dinner favourite.

INGREDIENTS

Serves 6-8

250g short crust pastry
600ml thick custard
4-5 tbsp. raspberry jam
1 large banana
1-2 tbsp. desiccated coconut

METHOD

1. Preheat the oven to 200ºC (390ºF, gas mark 6) and grease an 18cm by 10cm rectangular tin.
2. Line the tin with the pastry and bake it blind for 20-25 minutes until golden brown.
3. Allow the pastry to cool then spread the jam evenly over the base.
4. Slice the banana thinly and place on top of the jam.
5. Spoon over the custard and sprinkle with coconut.
6. Slice and serve.

This will keep covered in the fridge overnight, but no longer .

Chester Pudding

This a custard and almond based meringue pie. It is easier to make than a lemon meringue.

INGREDIENTS

Serves 6

200g shortcrust pastry
120g soft brown sugar
60g butter
½ teaspoon natural almond extract
30g ground almond
3 large eggs, separated
3 rounded tablespoons caster sugar

METHOD

1. Preheat the oven to 190ºC (375ºF, gas mark 5) and grease a round deep pie dish.
2. Roll out the pastry to fit the dish and bake blind for 10 minutes to 'set' the pastry.
3. Meanwhile put the sugar, butter, almonds and extract into a pan over a very low heat to melt the butter and allow the ingredients to mix well.
4. Remove from the heat and beat in the egg yolks. Return to a low heat and stir until it just thickens.
5. Spoon this mixture into the part baked pastry shell. Return to the oven and bake for 20 minutes.
6. Make a meringue topping by whisking the egg whites until stiff and forming peaks. I tend to add a small pinch of salt to the whites as it helps them retain the air. Sprinkle over a tablespoon of sugar at a time and whisk in quickly.
7. Spoon the meringue mixture over the top of the pie and bake for 10-15 minutes until the meringue is set and the peaks are golden brown.

Chorley Cakes

You can make one large or 6 small ones with this quantity. I prefer to make a big one and cut slices as I want them.

INGREDIENTS

300g shortcrust pastry
50g butter
30g soft brown sugar
Grated zest of 1 orange and 1 lemon
1 level tsp mixed spice
150g currants

For the topping:
1 egg white
2 tsp caster sugar

METHOD

1. Preheat the oven to 200ºC (390ºF, gas mark 6) and grease a large baking sheet. This will do for a large cake or 6 small ones.
2. Beat the butter, sugar, spice and fruit zest together until light and fluffy.
3. Add the currants and beat into the creamed mixture.
4. Roll out the pastry either into one large or six small rounds.
5. Spoon the filling into the centre of the rounds and bring up the edges to cover the filling. Pinch and seal the edges and lightly roll with a rolling pin to flatten into a round shape.
6. Place on the prepared baking sheet and brush with the egg white and sprinkle with sugar. Bake for 20 minutes if they are small ones or 30-35 minutes for a large one.

They can be eaten warm or cold and can be served with custard if you wish.

Marble Buns

I used to make these with my Aunt when I stayed at her house.

INGREDIENTS

Makes 12 buns

150g butter
150g golden caster sugar
2 eggs
1 tsp vanilla extract
150g self-raising flour
20g cocoa

METHOD

1. Place 12 paper muffin cases in a 12 hole muffin tin. Preheat the oven to 170C/gas mark 3.
2. Cream the butter and sugar together in a mixing bowl until fluffy and light.
3. Sift 1 tbsp of the flour into the mixture and beat in the eggs and vanilla.
4. Sift in the rest of the flour. Fold the flour into the creamed mixture.
5. Spoon a third of the mixture into a separate bowl and sift in the cocoa. Fold in gently.
6. Put a dessertspoon of the vanilla mixture into the muffin case and a heaped teaspoon of the chocolate mixture stir together so the mixture is streaked.
7. Bake for about 15 minutes until springy to the touch.

I like to ice these with plain white glacé icing and a streak of melted chocolate. Mix 80g of icing sugar with a little water until spoon able but not too runny and smooth on the top of the cakes. Melt about 50g dark chocolate in a bowl over a pan of hot water or in the microwave. Drizzle a little of the chocolate over the buns and streak with a cocktail stick.

Chapter 6

Northern Ireland

Most of today's traditional dishes herald not from the Irish nobility or the gentry but from the kitchens of farms. It is wholesome and usually locally sourced. Cooking methods were simple; cook pots over open fires were the major way of preparing meals. Griddles were used to make farls and breads and, my favourite, potato cakes.

Soups are a main dish on many British tables. Here are two of my favourite Irish recipes.

Irish Potato Soup

This is an easy soup to prepare and requires few ingredients. Traditionally it was pushed through a sieve to purée the soup, but I use a hand blender as I like it a bit chunky.

INGREDIENTS

Serves 6

30g butter
6 medium-sized potatoes, peeled and sliced or diced
1 large onion, chopped
1 litre vegetable stock
300ml milk
1 rounded tsp cornflour, mixed to a smooth paste with a little of the milk
1 tbsp fresh parsley, chopped
Salt and pepper to taste
A little grated nutmeg

METHOD

1. Melt the butter in a large lidded pan and add the potatoes and onion. Cook over a low heat and cover. Allow to sweat for about 10 minutes.
2. Add the stock and season with salt and pepper and nutmeg. Bring to the boil then reduce the heat and simmer gently until the vegetables are very soft.
3. Stir the cornflour mixture into the other milk and stir into the soup. Bring to the boil and then simmer for 2 minutes.
4. Blend to taste and stir in the parsley. Heat again if necessary before serving.

Serve with Irish wheaten bread.

Bacon and Savoy Cabbage Soup

A wonderfully easy soup that can be varied to suit the seasonality of vegetables – add a diced carrot and/or a stick of celery if you wish.

INGREDIENTS

Serves 4

300g chunky bacon, cut into bite-size pieces
2–3 potatoes, peeled and cut into cubes (depending on size)
1 small onion, chopped finely
400g can chopped tomatoes
600ml chicken or vegetable stock
300g savoy cabbage leaves, cut into thin strips
Salt and pepper to taste

METHOD

1. Cook the bacon in a large lidded pan over a medium heat until lightly browned all over. Pour away any excess fat if you wish.
2. Add the onion and potato and cook with the bacon for a few minutes.
3. Add the tomatoes and stock and bring to the boil. Reduce the heat and simmer for 20 minutes.
4. Add the cabbage and season to taste. Simmer for another 5–10 minutes.

Serve immediately or allow to cool and reheat to serve as necessary.

Irish Wheaten Soda Bread

INGREDIENTS

Makes 1 large round loaf

200g strong wholemeal flour
250g strong white flour
1 rounded tsp baking powder
1 level teaspoon baking soda
1 level tsp salt
1 rounded tsp sugar
280ml carton of buttermilk or 280ml milk with 1 tbsp lemon juice stirred in
2 tbsp. vegetable oil or melted butter

METHOD

1. Preheat the oven to 220°C (425°F, Gas 7) and grease a baking tray.
2. Sieve the white flour, salt and baking powder into a bowl.
3. Stir in the wholemeal flour and sugar until combined with the other ingredients.
4. Add the milk or buttermilk and the oil or butter. Stir well to combine all the ingredients. The mixture should be slightly sticky.
5. Bind with your hands but don't knead the dough. Form into a round.
6. Place it on the prepared baking sheet and flatten slightly. Cut deeply (about 2cm) across the top of the dough in both directions. This makes 4 sections.
7. Bake for 20–25 minutes until well risen and golden brown.

This bread may be eaten after cooling for 10 minutes.

To vary the flavour and add a healthy dose of oats to your bread, substitute 100g of wholemeal or white flour for 100g of medium rolled oats.

Add this to the mixture when you stir in the wholemeal flour. Continue in the same way as in the rest of the recipe.

Potato Farls

The word farl comes from the Gaelic word 'fardel', which means four sections. These can be made with leftover mash. I usually make extra so we can have them for breakfast.

INGREDIENTS

About 450g mashed potatoes

Salt to taste
25–30g plain flour
1 tbsp melted butter

METHOD

1. Put the potato into a bowl and sprinkle over the salt.
2. Add the melted butter and stir in.
3. Sift over sufficient flour to make a dough and combine well.
4. Lightly flour a work surface and a rolling pin then transfer the potato mixture to the floured surface. Use the rolling pin to flatten the dough into a circle measuring about ½ cm deep.
5. Cut into 4 equal sections. Heat a griddle or flat-based frying pan and cook without fat for 3 minutes each side.

Serve with soup or with butter on their own.

Irish Fry-up

A Saturday morning must-have.

INGREDIENTS

Serves 2

4 rashers bacon
4 Irish recipe sausages
2 large tomatoes
2–4 slices Irish black pudding or white pudding if you prefer
2 slices soda bread
2 potato farls
2 eggs
A little oil for frying

METHOD
1. Fry the bacon, soda bread and potato farls in the bacon fat and keep warm whilst you fry the sausage and black pudding.
2. Fry the tomatoes and then the eggs just before plating up.

Delicious!

Beef in Guinness

This is my version of a delicious dish we had with some Irish friends. This recipe is great served with mashed or baked potatoes and a green vegetable of your choice. It is an economical dish as it uses a cheap cut of meat – the Guinness tenderises it as it cooks slowly.

INGREDIENTS

Serves 4–6

20g lard or oil
1kg stewing beef, cut into cubes
2 tbsp flour, seasoned with salt and pepper
2 onions, sliced thinly
3 medium-sized carrots
500ml Guinness or 300ml and 200ml water
Salt and pepper to taste

METHOD

1. Preheat the oven to 180°C (350°F, Gas 4).
2. Toss the beef in the seasoned flour and fry gently in the fat or oil to just colour. Put the meat into a large lidded casserole dish.
3. Fry the onions in the same pan as the meat and add the carrots for a few minutes. Stir the onions and carrots into the meat.
4. Add a little of the Guinness to the frying pan and stir to release all the flavours from the bottom of the pan. Pour over the meat and vegetables.
5. Stir in the rest of the Guinness and cover with the lid.
6. Cook for 2 ½ hours, stirring and checking for seasoning halfway through the cooking time.

Champ

A combination of potatoes and spring onions makes a savoury accompaniment to any meat dish, or it can be served on its own.

INGREDIENTS

Serves 4

5–6 large potatoes, peeled and cut into chunks
8–10 spring onions or scallions, trimmed and sliced
Salt and pepper
120ml milk
25g butter

METHOD

1. Boil the potatoes until tender and poach the onions in the milk for about 5 minutes.
2. Mash the potatoes with salt and pepper and the butter.
3. Add the hot milk and onions and mix together.

Traditional Irish Stew

This is best made with mutton as the flavour is amazing and the long, slow cooking time is ideal. It is one of those meals that takes little preparation and gives no worries whilst cooking. It can be served straight from the pot and doesn't need any accompaniments, unless you fancy some pickled cabbage or onions.

INGREDIENTS

Serves 4–6

1kg mutton, cut from the bone into big chunks
4–5 large potatoes, sliced thickly
2 large onions, sliced
4 medium carrots
Salt and pepper
About 400ml water

METHOD

Preheat the oven to 190°C (375°F, Gas 5).
Place a layer of the potatoes at the bottom of a lidded casserole dish. Then add a layer of meat, then onions, then carrot and start with potato again. Do this until you end with a final potato layer. Season as you go and finish by pouring in the water.
Cook for 20 minutes, then turn the oven down to 150°C (300°F, Gas 2) and cook for 2 ½ hours.

If you wish, stir some fresh parsley into the water before adding to the stew.

Irish Whisky Cake

This was an old recipe of my friend's grandma, who was from Belfast. Her family made this for St Patrick's Day.

INGREDIENTS

Makes 8–10 portions

180g butter
180g golden caster sugar
2 medium eggs
220g self-raising flour
Zest of 1 lemon
50g currants
100g raisins
50g sultanas
20g mixed candied peel
50ml Irish whisky
½ level tsp cinnamon
A pinch nutmeg
2 tbsp. milk
1 tbsp. Demerara sugar for sprinkling over the top

METHOD

1. Grease and line an 18cm (7in) round tin. Preheat the oven to 180°C (350°F, Gas 4).
2. Put the fruit into a bowl and sprinkle over the whisky, stir well and leave to soak overnight.
3. Cream the butter and sugar together until very light and fluffy.
4. Add a tablespoon of the flour and beat in the eggs.
5. Sieve the flour and spices together into the creamed mixture and begin to fold in.
6. Add the lemon zest and dried fruit and finish folding

in all together.

7. Stir in the milk and spoon into the prepared tin. Sprinkle a little sugar over the top at this stage for a crispy topping.

8. Bake for 1–1 ½ hours until deep golden in colour.

9. Allow to cool in the tin for 10 minutes then transfer to a cooling rack and cool completely before slicing.

Barmbrack

This bread is a traditional bake at Halloween. It is baked containing various items but most commonly a golden ring to signify the forthcoming wedding of the person who was lucky enough to receive the slice with the ring. But if you are already married then I'm not quite sure what it means!

This is a slightly sweet and spicy fruity loaf that is great sliced and served with butter.

INGREDIENTS

5g fresh yeast
125ml warm milk
1 tsp sugar
280g plain flour
Pinch salt
1 level tsp mixed spice
A little grated nutmeg
200g mixed fruit
1 egg, beaten
50g butter
50g caster sugar

METHOD

1. Cream the yeast and sugar together with a little of the warm milk and leave to froth up in a warm place.
2. Sieve the flour, salt and spice together into a mixing bowl.
3. Rub the butter into the flour mixture and stir in the sugar.
4. Make a well in the centre of the flour and pour in the yeast mixture and the rest of the warm milk and the beaten egg.

5. Stir everything together, then use your hands to knead everything together. Start to knead the dough and as you do so add the fruit and knead it in. Knead for 5 more minutes.
6. Cover and leave to prove until the dough has doubled in size.
7. Knead the dough to knock back for 2–3 minutes. Shape into a round and then leave to rise for 30 minutes on a greased baking sheet. Preheat the oven to 200°C (400°F, Gas 6).
8. Bake for 35–40 minutes until deep golden in colour.
9. When it is baked and still very hot, brush the top with honey to glaze – this gives a nice shiny and sweet crust. Allow to cool before slicing and serving with butter.

Oaten Honeycomb Pudding

This is a pudding with a difference: it is a steamed, honey-flavoured pudding that contains no wheat flour but, as its name suggests, uses oats.

INGREDIENTS

Serves 6

450ml whole milk
180g porridge oats
50g golden caster sugar
30ml honey
30g butter
Zest of 1 orange
1 tsp ground cinnamon
3 eggs, separated

METHOD

Pour the milk into a heavy-based pan and bring to the boil. Stir in the oats and turn down the heat to a simmer. Cook for 5 minutes.
Beat in the sugar, honey, butter, orange zest and cinnamon. Remove from the heat.
Beat the egg yolks into the oat mixture.
Whisk the egg whites until they reach the stiff peak stage and fold into the pudding mixture.
Grease a large pudding basin with butter and pour in the pudding mixture.
Cover the basin with a piece of greaseproof paper, pleated in the centre to allow for the pudding to rise. Then cover with foil, doing the same pleat in the centre. Secure with string.
Steam for 2 ½ hours, checking water levels after every 30 minutes.

Hot Irish Punch

INGREDIENTS

For two people

½ lemon, sliced
6 whole cloves
1 teaspoon brown sugar
2 tots Irish whisky, as much as you like!
Hot water to top up the glass

METHOD

1. Warm 2 lemon tea type glass and add the lemon, 3 cloves per glass, ½ teaspoon sugar and the whisky.
2. Top up with hot water, stir and leave for a few minutes.
3. Remove the cloves if you wish and drink slowly in front of a large fire.

Chapter 7

The North East

A very dramatic and beautiful part of Britain, the North East has a wealth of rolling hills and moors, home to many sheep and cattle. The food isn't all Yorkshire pudding. The best fish and chips I ever tasted came from a small chip shop on the Yorkshire coast.

Northumberland has a flourishing kipper industry and in Craster, a fishing village not far from Alnwick, they have been smoking kippers in the original smokehouses for over 120 years. There are wonderful cheeses made in this region. Some of my favourites are Wensleydale, made in Hawes, Yorkshire Blue and Cotherstone, a yellow, tangy cheese from Teesdale.

Rhubarb is a traditional foodstuff grown in the 'Rhubarb Triangle', between Leeds, Pontefract and Wakefield.

Potted Kippers

This is a delicious snack or a perfect starter course. It is a quick and easy recipe.

INGREDIENTS

Serves 4

2 large kipper fillets, skinned and the flesh broken into small pieces
120g butter
100g cream cheese – the light version works just as well as the full fat
1 tbsp. lemon juice
Black pepper to taste
4 thin slices of lemon to decorate the top

METHOD

1. Melt 20g of the butter in a small pan over a gentle heat and stir in the cream cheese, lemon juice and black pepper.
2. Add the fish flakes and blend in well with a wooden spoon. The fish flakes should break up into the butter mixture.
3. Turn off the heat and transfer the mixture to four individual ramekins or one serving dish.
4. Smooth out the top with a palette knife.
5. Melt the rest of the butter and pour over the top of the kipper pâté.
6. Top with the slices of lemon and place in the fridge to set for at least 30 minutes. Serve with slices of hot toast.

Kipper Quiche

This a tasty flan that can be served with salad and crusty bread. This can be made in one large flan case or you can make four individual ones.

INGREDIENTS

Serves 4

250g shortcrust pastry
Approximately 200g kipper fillets
2 eggs
300ml milk
1 tbsp. of fresh or 1 level tsp dried parsley

METHOD

1. Preheat the oven to 200°C (400°F, Gas 6) and grease a 20cm (8in) flan tin or four small ones.
2. Roll out the pastry to fit the flan tin and line the prepared tin with the pastry. Place a piece of greaseproof paper, cut to make a circle about 4cm larger than the tin, over the pastry shell and weigh down with baking beads or dried beans.
3. Bake in the oven for 15 minutes.
4. Prepare the kippers by skinning and checking for any bones. Leave the flesh in bite-size pieces.
5. When the pastry shell is cooked it won't be fully baked but it will be 'set'. Spread the kippers over the pastry base.
6. Whisk the egg with the milk and pour over the kippers.
7. Sprinkle the top with the parsley.
8. Put the quiche on a baking sheet and bake for about 30 minutes or until the filling has set.

Pease Pudding

This is traditionally made with ham or bacon but my friends make it as a vegetarian dish. It can be eaten with cooked ham and bacon or served with a roast dinner.

INGREDIENTS

Serves 4–6

450g dried split peas
60g butter
1 egg, beaten
Salt for seasoning
Black pepper to taste

METHOD

1. Cover the dried peas with cold water, leaving a free depth of 3cm as the peas will swell. Leave to soak overnight or do this early in the morning for an evening meal. They need between 7 and 8 hours to soak.
2. After soaking, drain the peas and put in fresh cold water to just cover them and bring to the boil.
3. Turn down the heat and simmer for 1 hour. Preheat the oven to 180°C (350°F, Gas 4).
4. Drain the peas and put back in the pan. Mash the peas with the butter and the egg, season with salt and black pepper and mix well together.
5. Transfer the peas to a buttered pudding basin and cover with foil.
6. Stand the basin on a baking tray and bake in the oven for 25–30 minutes.

Serve in wedges.

Northumberland Casserole

You could try serving the pease pudding with this tasty casserole.

INGREDIENTS

Serves 4

350g lamb's liver, washed and sliced
2 tbsp. flour, seasoned with salt and pepper
2 tbsp. oil or 15g lard
2 large onions, sliced thinly
8 rashers bacon, chopped into bite-size pieces
1kg potatoes, peeled and cut into slices
300ml beef stock

METHOD

1. Boil the potatoes until tender.
2. Dip the slices of liver in the seasoned flour, heat the oil or lard in a frying pan and fry the liver on both sides. Place in a casserole dish.
3. Fry the onions in the same pan and oil as the liver for 2 minutes then add the potatoes. Fry for 2–3 minutes.
4. Lay the onions and potatoes on top of the liver and sprinkle with the bacon pieces.
5. Pour the stock over the casserole and cover with a lid or foil.
6. Place in the oven at 190°C (375°F, Gas 5) for 35–40 minutes.

Cidered Fish Casserole

You can use any firm white fish for this recipe. You can also use any cheese you fancy – I like it with crumbly Wensleydale. It can be served with boiled new potatoes or thick chips.

INGREDIENTS

Serves 4

500g haddock, cod, pollack or similar fish fillets, skinned
4 ripe tomatoes
50g closed-cup mushrooms, sliced
150ml dry cider
50g breadcrumbs
50g grated cheese
Salt and pepper to taste

METHOD

1. Cut the fish into 3cm pieces and lay them in the bottom of a buttered casserole dish.
2. Put a layer of tomatoes on top, then the mushrooms and repeat until they are all used up.
3. Season with salt and pepper and pour over the cider.
4. Cover and cook in the oven at 190°C (375°F, Gas 5) for 20 minutes.
5. Remove the lid and sprinkle over the breadcrumbs and then the cheese.
6. Place under a hot grill and allow the topping to brown and bubble.

Yorkshire Parkin

This reminds me of our time at college in Leeds, a slice of parkin and a cheese pasty made up my lunch from the local bakers shop.

INGREDIENTS

This recipe is sufficient to make 12 squares.

130g self-raising flour
1 level tsp ground ginger
130g fine oatmeal
2 tbsp black treacle
2 tbsp golden syrup
50g brown sugar
50g butter
1 egg
2 tbsp milk

METHOD

1. Grease a 15cm (6in) square tin and preheat the oven to 170°C (340°F, Gas 3).
2. Sieve the ginger with the flour into a large mixing bowl.
3. Melt the butter with the treacle, syrup and sugar together in a pan over a very low heat. As soon as the butter has melted, remove from the heat, stir well and beat in the egg.
4. Pour the buttery mixture into the flour and mix vigorously with a wooden spoon.
5. Add the milk and beat again – it should be a soft, easily poured mixture. If not add another tablespoon of milk.

6. Pour the mixture into the tin and bake for 50–55 minutes. It should be firm to the touch in the centre when cooked. If not, bake for 5 more minutes.
7. Allow to cool in the tin on a cooling rack. After 10 minutes of cooling, cut the cake into 12 equal squares.
8. When cool, lift the squares out of the tin and transfer to an airtight container. This develops a stickiness if left for 24 hours before eating and the flavour is better. So make this the day before you want to eat it.

Stottie Cakes

These are made from bread-type dough and are real Geordie treats. They are traditionally split in half and served with thick slices of ham or pease pudding.

INGREDIENTS

Makes 6–8 depending on the size you wish

500g strong plain flour
1 tsp salt
30g butter
1 x 7g sachet of fast-action dried yeast
Approximately 280ml warm milk

METHOD

1. Sieve together the flour and salt into a mixing bowl.
2. Stir in the yeast and rub in the butter.
3. Mix in the warm milk, sufficient to make a soft but pliable dough.
4. Knead well with the hands to combine and carry on kneading for 10 minutes.
5. Leave the dough to prove for about 30 minutes in a warm place.
6. Preheat the oven to 220°C (425°F, Gas 7) and grease a baking tray. Turn the dough out onto a floured surface and knead again, knocking out all the air. Continue for a few minutes.
7. Break off small pieces of dough and roll out to flat cakes about 1.5cm deep. Make a dent in the centre of each with a spoon.
8. Put each cake on the baking tray and prick with a fork about four times.
9. Bake for 12–15 minutes until golden brown.
10. Cool for 10–15 minutes before eating.

Singing Hinnies

These are fruity cakes that are made on a griddle or in a flat frying pan but they can also be made in a hot oven. The singing bit comes from the sound they make whilst cooking and the hinny bit is from the word 'honey' which is used as a term of affection.

INGREDIENTS

Makes 8–10

350g self-raising flour
2 tsp baking powder
50g ground rice
1 level tsp salt
50g butter
75g currants
150ml single cream mixed with 2 tbsp. milk

METHOD

1. Preheat the oven to 190°C (375°F, Gas 5). Sieve the salt, baking powder and flour together into a bowl and stir in the ground rice.
2. Rub in the butter until the mixture resembles breadcrumbs.
3. Stir in the currants.
4. Make a well in the centre and pour in the cream. Stir to make a soft dough.
5. Use your hands to make flat patties about 5mm thick and 5cm in diameter.
6. Prick them all over with a fork. Now either place on a greased baking sheet and bake for 10–15 minutes or cook on a greased hot griddle or in a flat frying pan for 3–4 minutes on each side.
7. Serve hot, split open with butter.

Curd Tarts

Another of my all time favourites from my college days. There are several good recipes for curd tarts but this is the easiest and my favourite. Make your own curds as it doesn't taste as good made with shop bought cottage cheese.

Easy curds for your tart.
This makes more curd than you need, but you can eat the other as cottage cheese and mix in some chopped chives, smoked salmon or use it in a cheese cake.

You will need:
1 litre whole milk
2 tablespoons lemon juice
A large pan
A piece of muslin or cheese cloth
A small sieve or colander
Another pan or large bowl to catch the whey

METHOD

1. Heat the milk in a pan until almost boiling then remove from the heat.
2. Stir in the lemon juice and return to a low heat for 2-3 minutes.
3. Place the muslin or cheesecloth over the colander or sieve in a bowl or pan. Pour the curds and whey through the cloth, catching all the curds. Don't be tempted to squeeze the curds, let it drip naturally.
4. Hang up on a hook or tie onto a tap over the bowl or pan and allow to go completely cold. Once cold most of the whey will have drained away.
5. Transfer the curd to a clean bowl and cut into them.
6. Strain away any more whey and the curds are ready to use in your recipe.

7. Any unused curd will keep in a covered container for 3-4 days especially if you add a little salt.

To make the tart:

INGREDIENTS
200g shortcrust pastry
250g curds
60g currants
60g soft brown sugar
2 tablespoons double cream
2 eggs, beaten well
Grated zest of half a lemon and 1 tablespoon juice
A pinch grated nutmeg

METHOD

1. Preheat the oven to 200C/gas mark 6 and grease a 20cm diameter pie or flan dish.
2. Line the prepared dish with the pastry and bake blind for 15 minutes until set. Turn the oven down to 180C/gas mark 4.
3. Place the curds in a mixing bowl with the fruit and stir.
4. Stir in the cream and sugar.
5. Beat in the eggs, lemon zest and juice.
6. Spoon the curd mixture into the pastry shell and sprinkle with a little nutmeg.
7. Bake for about 20 minutes until set and golden on the top.

Best eaten cold.

Yorkshire Pudding

This is of course synonymous with roast beef but we have it with most roasts and, if there is any left over, I like it spread with jam or sprinkled with lemon juice and golden syrup. The batter can be used for making toad-in-the-hole as well. I find this is best prepared with an electric hand whisk.

INGREDIENTS

Serves 6

180g plain flour
½ level tsp salt
2 eggs, beaten
190ml milk
100ml water
25g lard or 2 tbsp sunflower oil, lard or other animal fat; duck or goose gives best results as it gets much hotter than oil so gives a crisper finish.

METHOD

1. Preheat the oven to 220°C (425°F, Gas 7).
2. Place the lard or oil in a roasting pan.
3. Sieve the flour and salt together into a mixing bowl.
4. Make a well in the centre of the flour and pour in the eggs. Use a whisk to begin beating in the eggs.
5. Combine the milk and water together and add a little of the milk mixture to the flour and eggs. Whisk and keep adding the milk, gradually whisking all the time.
6. When all the milk has been incorporated into the flour, whisk for another minute.
7. Put the roasting pan containing the fat or oil into the oven for a few minutes until it gets very hot.
8. Carefully lift out the pan and pour the pudding

mixture straight in.
9.   Put the pan back in the oven and cook for 35–40
     minutes or until it is golden and well risen.

Chapter 8

Scotland

Scottish cooking is much more than just fried Mars bars, it is wonderfully varied and rich. Since the distance between the coasts in Scotland is much shorter than anywhere in the country, the sea food is wonderful. Perhaps more than anything, Scotland is a maritime country. Almost all the major cities are on or near the coast.

There is also a long history of game and, in particular, grouse and venison, mainly shot by rich people who came to own vast tracts of the countryside, keeping all but the wealthy away, often quite violently.

For me, Scottish food is exemplified by oats, a grain that grows well in cooler conditions and is remarkably good for you. Everyone should eat more oats!

Scotch Broth

INGREDIENTS

Serves 4-6

700g of any cheap cut of lamb or mutton, with any excess fat removed. If the meat has some bones in, use 100g more
1.5 litres water
130g pearl barley
150g dried peas, soaked overnight
25g butter
1 medium-sized onion, chopped
1 leek, sliced thinly
1 small turnip, chopped
2-3 carrots, diced
A handful of shredded cabbage
1 tbsp. freshly chopped parsley
2 sprigs thyme
Salt and pepper. I prefer white pepper because of the kick it gives to the broth

METHOD

1. Place the meat in the water with the salt and pepper and bring to the boil. Once boiling reduce the heat to a gentle simmer. Cover and cook for 2 - 3 hours until the meat is tender. Skim off any fat from the surface.
2. When the meat is cooked, lift it out and pour the stock into another vessel for later. Remove any bones and chop up the meat into small chunks about 1cm in size.
3. Melt the butter in the pan used for cooking the meat and fry the onion, leek, carrots and turnip gently for 5 minutes.
4. Add the barley, herbs and drained peas and pour over the stock from the meat.

5. Bring to the boil then reduce the heat and simmer for 1 hour until the peas are tender.
6. Add a little more water if the soup is too thick during the cooking time.

This is delicious served with soda bread.

Cullen Skink

Traditionally, Finnan haddock was used in this, but as this is hard to come by use ordinary smoked haddock. The natural undyed fish is best.

Finnan haddock was used by the villagers of Cullen on the north-east coast of Scotland, near Aberdeen. They used it to make their broth or 'skink'. It is a very rich tasting dish, definitely more than a soup.

INGREDIENTS

Serves 4-6

450g smoked haddock
1 onion, chopped
600ml of water, or fish/chicken stock
3 small leeks
220g potatoes, boiled and mashed
50g butter
300ml single cream
1 egg yolk
Salt and pepper
2 tbsp. chopped fresh parsley

METHOD

1. Put the fish and the onions in a saucepan and just cover with water. Bring slowly to the boil, then simmer gently for about 8 minutes.
2. Remove the fish from the liquor and strain it, reserving all of the cooking liquid. Discard the onion and bones etc.
3. Flake the fish, remove any bones or skin.
4. Put the fish cooking liquid and stock in a pan and

bring to the boil.

5. Add the leeks and simmer until they are tender.

6. Turn the heat down to a gentle simmer. Add the mashed potato and butter and stir in the flaked fish.

7. Beat the egg yolk into the cream and stir this into the soup. Season with salt and pepper to taste and simmer very gently for 2 minutes.

8. Serve in bowls with some fresh parsley sprinkled on top.

Partan Pie

This is a crab pie made in the shell. It makes an unusual starter or lunch dish.

INGREDIENTS

Serves 2-4

1 dressed crab or 450g mixed brown and white crabmeat
Salt and pepper
½ tsp nutmeg
3 tbsp. white wine vinegar
2 tbsp. Dijon mustard
100g fresh brown breadcrumbs
2 tbsp. butter

METHOD

1. Mix all the crabmeat together with the salt and nutmeg.
2. Heat the vinegar and mustard together in a small saucepan.
3. Put the crabmeat back in the shell if you have one, if not put it into a shallow dish.
4. Pour the vinegar over the meat and sprinkle with the breadcrumbs.
5. Dot the top with the butter and brown under a hot grill.

Herrings in Oatmeal

This dish goes back to when the scholars with little money would take a sack of oatmeal with them from the Highlands to St Andrews University. The oats would help sustain them through their studies. They would buy a few herrings to mix with their oatmeal to add variety to what would have been a very boring diet.

INGREDIENTS

Serves 4-6

6 filleted herrings
Salt and pepper
100g coarse oatmeal
100g butter or bacon fat
1 tbsp chopped parsley
1 lemon sliced

METHOD

1. Season the fish with salt and pepper and place the oatmeal on a plate.
2. Roll the fish in the oatmeal. Coat well, it will stick as the fish are oily.
3. Heat the butter or bacon fat in a large frying pan until it sizzles. Fry the fish for about 3 minutes on both sides.
4. When they are crispy, serve sprinkled with parsley and the lemon slices.

Scottish Collops

These are thin slices of meat, either venison, lamb or beef, or a mixture. They are cooked in the oven with onions and mushrooms.

INGREDIENTS

Serves 4

700g lamb or beef steak cut into ½ cm thick by about 5cm
25g seasoned flour
50g butter
1 onion, sliced
200g open cup mushrooms
400ml beef stock

METHOD

1. Preheat the oven to 180°C (350°F, Gas 4).
2. Melt the butter in a frying pan and gently fry the onions.
3. After about 3 minutes add the mushrooms and cook for 5 minutes.
4. Put the vegetables in a lidded casserole dish.
5. Dip the pieces of meat in the seasoned flour and coat well.
6. Add a little more butter to the frying pan if necessary and fry the collops of meat on both sides for about 2 minutes each side.
7. Lay them on top of the mushrooms and onions.
8. Heat the stock if it is cold and pour over the casserole. Season to taste.
9. Cover with a lid and cook for about 50 minutes to 1 hour.

Serve with creamed potatoes and steamed or boiled cabbage.

Scotch Eggs

These were often eaten as part of the breakfast; we tend to eat them cold with a picnic or salad meal.

INGREDIENTS
Serves 6

6 eggs, hard-boiled and shelled
350g sausage meat
1 dessertspoon of parsley
1 tsp dried sage
½ tsp grated nutmeg
Salt and pepper
1 egg, beaten
120g breadcrumbs
Sunflower oil for deep frying

METHOD

1. Put the sausage meat in a bowl with the parsley, sage and nutmeg. Add salt and pepper to taste. Mix well with your hands.
2. Divide the sausage meat into 6 equal sections. Form each section into a round and mould it around the eggs.
3. Roll the covered eggs in the beaten egg and coat in the breadcrumbs. Have all the Scotch eggs ready to cook before heating the oil.
4. Heat the oil until very hot. If using a deep fat fryer ensure it has reached 190°C. Carefully put the eggs in the oil and fry for 4-5 minutes, turning them as they cook so they brown evenly. Cook no more than 3 eggs at a time.
5. Drain the cooked eggs on kitchen paper.

Mutton Pie

You can use mutton or lamb for this recipe; make sure the meat is well trimmed of fat.

INGREDIENTS

Serves 6

1kg mutton or lamb, cut into 2cm cubes
2 tbsp. oil
2 large onions, chopped
450g turnips, peeled and sliced thickly
300ml warm stock or water
1 level tsp dried or 1 tsp freshly chopped rosemary
1 tbsp. chopped parsley
1 tbsp. plain flour
Salt and pepper
225g rough puff pastry

METHOD

1. Fry the meat and onions together in a large lidded pan for 4-5 minutes, turning everything so the meat fries evenly.
2. Add the turnips and cook for 3 more minutes.
3. Add the herbs and season to taste.
4. Pour in the stock or water and stir. Allow to simmer, then cover with the lid and cook at simmering for 2 hours – check the liquid levels and add a little more if necessary.
5. Add the flour to 2 tablespoons of water and stir into the meat mixture, bring to the boil stirring constantly and turn down to simmering. Cook at simmering for a further 15 minutes.
6. Preheat the oven to 200°C (400°F, Gas 6).
7. Pour the pie filling into a deep pie dish and roll out

the pastry to fit the top. Allow the filling to cool for 10 minutes or the pastry won't rise and will become soggy, then cover the meat with the pastry, making a slit in the centre for the steam to escape.

8. Bake for 35-40 minutes until the pastry has risen and is golden and flaky.

Serve immediately with boiled new potatoes and garden peas.

Clootie Dumpling

This is a very easy pudding to prepare and is traditionally served at Hogmanay when 'first-footers' or visitors on New Year's Day are given a slice of the dumpling with a dram. I like it served with custard or brandy sauce.

INGREDIENTS
Serves 6

75g self-raising flour
75g white breadcrumbs
100g suet
100g caster sugar
50g sultanas
50g currants
50g raisins
1 tbsp. marmalade
1 level tsp mixed spice
1 tbsp. treacle
1 egg, beaten
150ml milk

METHOD
1. Butter a 1 litre pudding basin.
2. Mix all the ingredients together in a large mixing bowl until it forms a dough – I find it easier to use my hands.
3. Spoon the dough into the basin and cover with a layer of greaseproof paper secured with string, then a layer of foil.
4. Place in a steamer and steam for 3 hours, keep checking the water levels in the steamer base.
5. Serve hot or cold.

Slices of cold dumpling can be fried in a little butter and sprinkled with caster sugar.

Flummery

This is a creamy citrus flavoured dessert.

INGREDIENTS

Serves 6

3 heaped tbsp. fine oatmeal
Juice and zest of 2 oranges
2 tbsp. caster sugar
120ml single cream
1 tbsp. honey
2 tbsp. whisky

METHOD

1. Soak the oatmeal in enough cold water to cover with 2cm to spare. Leave overnight. Pour off the water and cover with a litre of fresh cold water. Leave for 24 hours.
2. Stir well and strain the liquid into a saucepan. Stir in the orange juice and sugar and bring to the boil.
3. Allow to boil for 8-10 minutes until it thickens.
4. Allow to cool until it is just warm then stir in the cream, honey and whisky.

Spoon into dishes or tall glasses and top with the orange zest. Chill until set. Serve with another dollop of thick cream.

The whisky may be omitted if you wish or replaced with brandy.

Haggis with Barley

This is the fundamental Scottish dish that is cooked in a stomach. The basic ingredients are offal, oats and barley with onion. I am sure that many of you won't with this haggis recipe but that's OK, it works for me and there are so many secret recipes out there that who knows what a haggis really is? Besides, I think they were kept a secret to stop people from knowing what horrid things go into them. Not so much a real secret, more a continuous changing of the subject.

INGREDIENTS

1 sheep's pluck (lungs and heart combined) which sometimes has the liver too, otherwise add 500g (1.1 lb) liver
500g (1.1 lb) beef suet
2 large finely chopped onions
1kg (1.1 lb) oatmeal
250g pearl barley

SEASONING
25g (5 level tsp) salt
1 tsp freshly ground black pepper
½ tsp cayenne
½ tsp allspice
⅛ tsp nutmeg
1 tsp ground mace

METHOD

1. Chop the pluck, all the meat, and give it a good wash. I would leave out the trachea, but some cut it up and grind it.
2. Start the onions frying in a little oil then add the meat and all the other ingredients except the oats and barley. Cover with water and bring to the boil,

simmering, adding more boiling water if necessary.

3. When the meat is tender and well cooked, add the barley. A knob of butter will deal with any scum – you want a wet mixture.

4. Once the whole mix has finished cooking and the barley is soft, stir in the oats. You are looking to create a mixture that is neither runny nor too dry.

5. Knot the skin and stuff with a spoon to create a strongly-packed sausage that is pressed down by twisting. Knot the other end very strongly and boil the haggis for 30 minutes, or put it in a moderate oven. This is to cook the oats and make a homogenous sausage.

Venison Pie

This is a really rich flavoured dish. It goes down a great on cold autumnal days. It only has a pastry lid and the meat is cooked separately, so it can be cooked the day before and the pie assembled in no time the next day.

INGREDIENTS

Serves 4

1 large onion, finely sliced
1 tbsp. vegetable oil
400g venison meat, cut into cubes
300g lean braising steak, cut into cubes
2 rounded tbsp. plain flour, seasoned with salt and pepper
300ml stock or water
150ml red wine
1 tbsp. tomato purée
1 tsp fresh thyme leaves
300g shortcrust pastry

METHOD
1. Fry the onion in the oil gently until translucent, do this in a sturdy lidded saucepan.
2. Toss all the meat in the seasoned flour and add to the onion fry for a few minutes, stirring so as the flour doesn't burn.
3. Pour in the stock and wine and stir well
4. Add the tomato purée and thyme leaves and simmer gently with the lid on for about 1 1/2 hours. Stir occasionally so as the gravy doesn't catch on the bottom of the pan.
5. Pour the meat into a deep pie dish.
6. Roll out the pastry so as it fits the top of the dish, about 1cm thick.
7. Place the pastry on top of the meat and make 3 slits

in the pastry so the steam can escape whilst it cooks.
8. Bake at 200/ gas mark 6 for around 25 minutes or until the pastry is golden brown. If the meat is cold bake for at least 40 minutes at 190C/gas mark 5.

Rabbit Fricassee

A delicious way of serving rabbit, an under used meat in my mind.

INGREDIENTS

Serves 4

1 large rabbit, jointed
Salt and pepper to taste
1 onion, chopped
1 smallish turnip, diced
2 medium carrots, chopped
1 tbsp. fresh parsley, chopped
2 sprigs fresh thyme
1 bay leaf
Water to just cover the rabbit
 For the sauce:
25 g butter kneaded together with 25g plain flour
300ml of the rabbit stock
2 tbsp. dry sherry
80ml double cream
Salt and pepper to taste

METHOD
1. Put the rabbit joints in a pan with some salt and pepper and pour over sufficient water to just cover. Bring to the boil then add the vegetables and herbs. Simmer for 1 hour
2. Pour 300 ml of the stock into a jug. Remove the meat from the bones. Put the meat and strained vegetables in a deep dish. Keep warm.
3. Make the sauce by putting the rabbit stock and sherry in a saucepan with the kneaded butter and flour mixture. Bring to the boil whisking continuously. Then simmer for 2 minutes.
4. Remove from the heat and stir in the cream and add

any more seasoning to taste.
5. Pour the sauce over the rabbit and serve
    immediately.